XTREME CARS

CORVETTE

A&D Xtreme
BOLD HI-LO NONFICTION
An imprint of Abdo Publishing
abdobooks.com

JOHN HAMILTON

TAKE IT TO THE XTREME!

GET READY FOR AN XTREME ADVENTURE! THE PAGES OF THIS BOOK WILL TAKE YOU INTO THE THRILLING WORLD OF CORVETTES. WHEN YOU HAVE FINISHED READING THIS BOOK, TAKE THE XTREME CHALLENGE ON PAGE 45 ABOUT WHAT YOU'VE LEARNED!

ABDOBOOKS.COM
Published by Abdo Publishing, a division of ABDO, PO Box 398166, Minneapolis, Minnesota 55439.

052022
092022

THIS BOOK CONTAINS RECYCLED MATERIALS

Editor: Sue Hamilton; Copy Editor: Tamara Britton

Graphic Design: John Hamilton

Cover Design: Laura Graphenteen

Cover Photo: Shutterstock

Interior Photos & Illustrations: Alamy-pgs 10-11, 18, 27; General Motors-pgs 1, 4-5, 8-9, 12-13, 14-15, 16-17, 19, 20-21, 22, 23, 24-25, 26, 27 28-29, 30-31, 32-33, 34-35, 36, 37, 38-39, 40, 41, 42-43, 44; Canadian Navy-pg 12.

LIBRARY OF CONGRESS CONTROL NUMBER: 2021942645

PUBLISHER'S CATALOGING-IN-PUBLICATION DATA

Names: Hamilton, John, author.

Title: Corvette / by John Hamilton

Description: Minneapolis, Minnesota : Abdo Publishing, 2023 | Series: Xtreme cars | Includes online resources and index.

Identifiers: ISBN 9781532196058 (lib. bdg.) | ISBN 9781098216986 (ebook)

Subjects: LCSH: Corvette automobile--Juvenile literature. | Sports cars--Juvenile literature. | Cars (Automobiles)--Juvenile literature.

Classification: DDC 629.2221--dc23

TABLE OF CONTENTS

CHAPTER 1

AMERICA'S SPORTS CAR

The 2021 Chevrolet Corvette.

The Chevrolet Corvette is often called "America's sports car." Built in the United States, this two-seater combines road thrills with stunning good looks. Since 1953, it has competed at a budget price with the best sports cars from Europe and Asia.

For more than 65 years, the 'Vette has changed with the times, but it has never failed to thrill car enthusiasts.

XTREME FACT

Chevrolet is also called Chevy. It is a division of General Motors, the Detroit, Michigan-based automotive company.

Eight generations of a classic American sports car, from the 1953 C1 model (far left) to the 2021 eighth-generation Corvette.

Car buffs were blown away when the redesigned 2020-2021 Corvette appeared in showrooms. It features a V-8 engine placed in the midsection of the car. It propels the Corvette from zero to 60 mph (97 kph) in a heart-stopping 2.9 seconds.

2020 eighth-generation Corvettes.

CHAPTER 2

DESIGNING A CLASSIC SPORTS CAR

Many of the most popular European sports cars were made by MG. In the early 1950s, the British company produced a line of T-series sports cars that were sold in the United States.

Millions of American soldiers returned home after the end of World War II. Many of them loved European sports cars. The soldiers began importing these small, fast cars. They enjoyed driving them on American roads and racetracks.

General Motors decided to build an American sports car. In 1951, the secret effort was called Project Opel. Later, Chevrolet's assistant advertising manager, Myron Scott, named the car "Corvette," after the speedy warships of World War II. The name was meant to be easily recognized by American soldiers.

A WWII-era corvette warship

XTREME FACT

The Corvette was the brainchild of famed General Motors chief designer Harley Earl. He was skilled at making sketches and clay models to design automobiles.

CHAPTER 3

FIRST GENERATION

The first Corvette was a **concept car**. It was shown at the General Motors Motorama auto show in New York City, New York, in 1953. The response from the public was so good it was rushed into production. That first year, it came in one color scheme: Polo White, with a Sportsman Red interior.

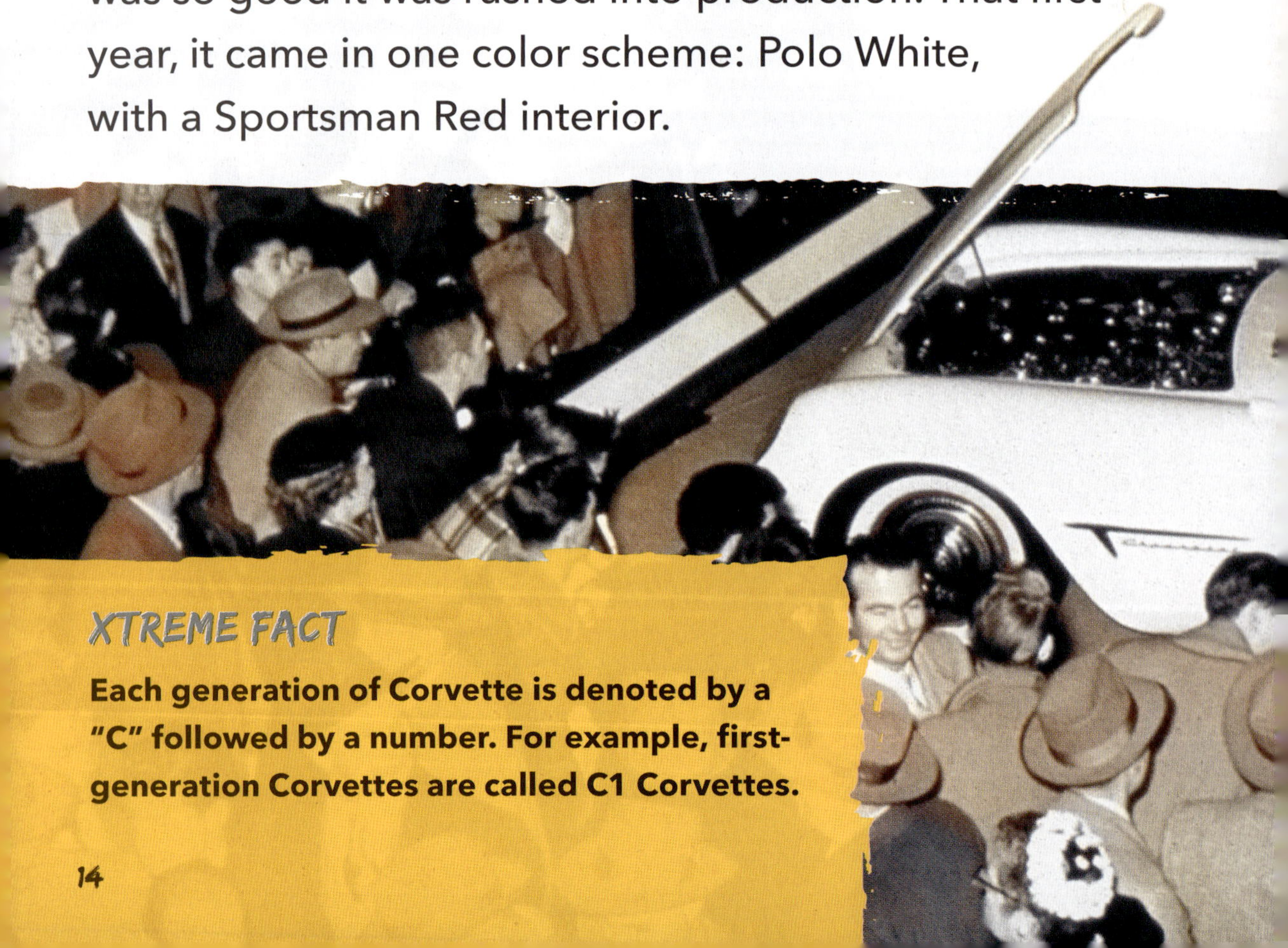

XTREME FACT

Each generation of Corvette is denoted by a "C" followed by a number. For example, first-generation Corvettes are called C1 Corvettes.

C1 SPECIFICATIONS

YEARS PRODUCED
1953-1962

MAXIMUM HORSEPOWER
150 (1953 model)

ZERO TO 60 MPH (97 KPH)
11.5 seconds (1953 model)

People liked the 1953 Corvette convertible's styling. However, it was underpowered. It had a modest six-**cylinder** engine and a two-speed automatic **transmission**. Only 300 C1 Corvettes were sold during the first year of production. In following years, its engine was beefed up to eight cylinders.

XTREME FACT

The first Corvettes were made in Flint, Michigan. Production was moved to St. Louis, Missouri, in December 1953. In 1981, production moved to its current location in Bowling Green, Kentucky.

CHAPTER 4

FIBERGLASS BODY PANELS

The Chevrolet Corvette was the first mass-produced car with a fiberglass body. Fiberglass is a plastic material reinforced with glass fibers. In 1953, it was easier and cheaper than sheet metal to form into the Corvette's curvy shape. The rustproof material is also lighter than metal. It makes the sports car faster and nimbler.

A man lifts a fiberglass body panel next to a C1 Corvette.

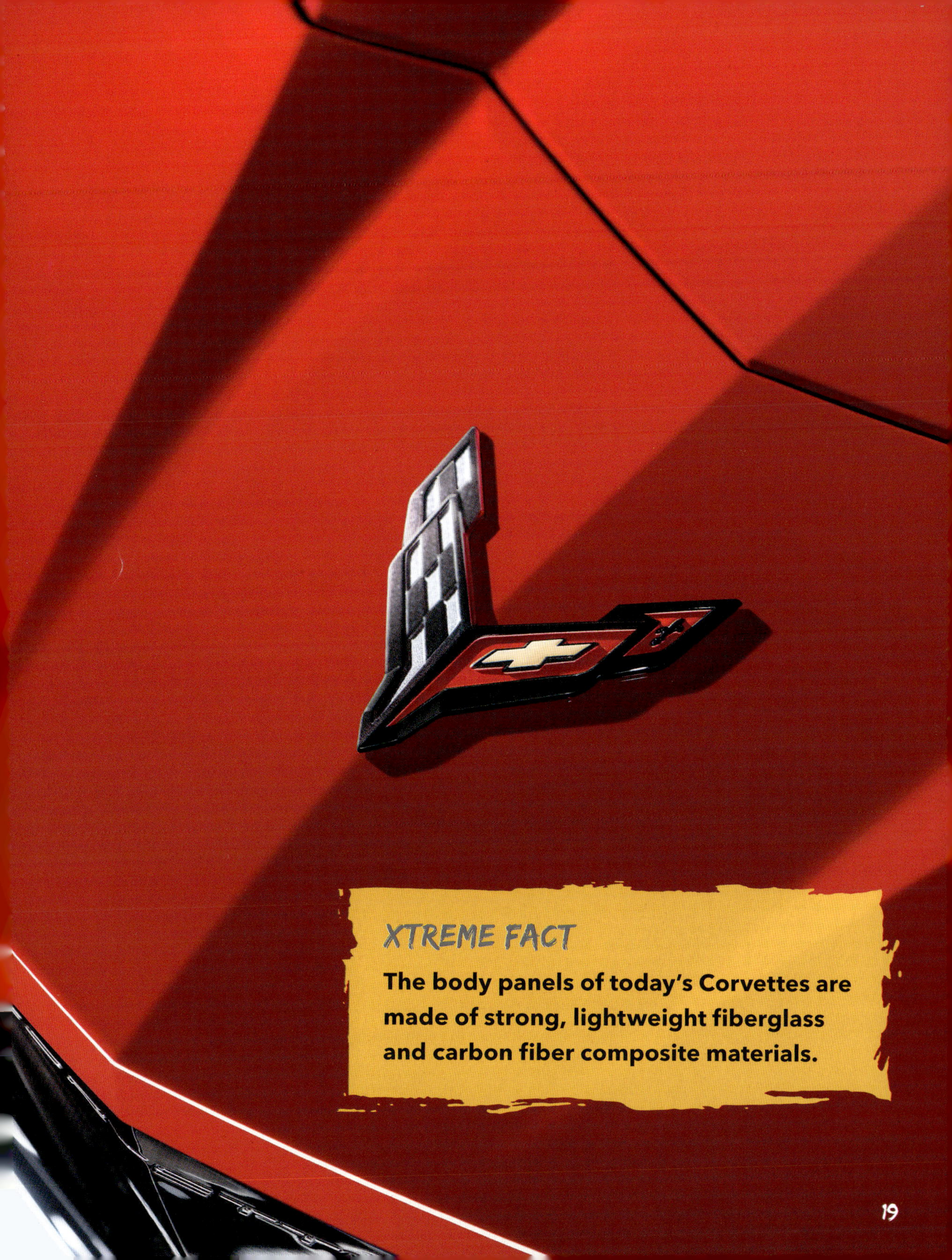

XTREME FACT

The body panels of today's Corvettes are made of strong, lightweight fiberglass and carbon fiber composite materials.

CHAPTER 5

SECOND GENERATION

In 1963, Chevrolet changed the Corvette so it could compete with European sports cars such as Porsche and Ferrari. It was redesigned by Bill Mitchell, Larry Shinoda, and Zora Arkus-Duntov.

C2 SPECIFICATIONS

YEARS PRODUCED
1963-1967

MAXIMUM HORSEPOWER
360 (1963 model)

ZERO TO 60 MPH (97 KPH)
5.8 seconds (1963 model)

The Corvette Sting Ray had more power and better handling. It had a powerful V-8 engine, hideaway headlamps, and **independent suspension** for better road handling. It came in both convertible and **coupe** versions.

XTREME FACT

The 1963 Corvette Sting Ray had a special split rear window. Although stylish, it made it hard to see out the back. Today, the model is cherished by Corvette collectors.

This was the first time Corvette was offered in a hardtop. The C2 Corvette was so radically different that it was given a new name, the Corvette Sting Ray. In later model years, Sting Ray was shortened to Stingray.

CHAPTER 6

THIRD GENERATION

The C3 Corvettes are often called the "Shark" generation. They were inspired by an earlier **concept car** called the "Mako Shark." They featured new body styling and a higher-performance engine.

C3 SPECIFICATIONS

YEARS PRODUCED
1968-1982

MAXIMUM HORSEPOWER
435 (1968 model)

ZERO TO 60 MPH (97 KPH)
6.1 seconds (1968 model)

CHAPTER 7

FOURTH GENERATION

Chevrolet released the C4 Corvette in 1984. It was a complete redesign in both body styling and mechanical engineering. Its clamshell-style hood was longer and lower. The tail length was shortened. The car was also wider, and had reduced flair in the fenders.

C4 SPECIFICATIONS

YEARS PRODUCED
1984-1996

MAXIMUM HORSEPOWER
205 (1984 model)

ZERO TO 60 MPH (97 KPH)
7.0 seconds (1984 model)

XTREME FACT

In 1992, the one-millionth Corvette was made. It was a white convertible, with a red interior, the same color scheme as the first Corvettes of 1953.

CHAPTER 8

FIFTH GENERATION

The C5 Corvettes arrived in 1997. They brought improvements in power, road handling, and driver comfort. A more rigid frame, and wheels that were farther apart, resulted in a better ride. A muscular LS1 eight-**cylinder** engine had much more power than the previous C4 Corvettes.

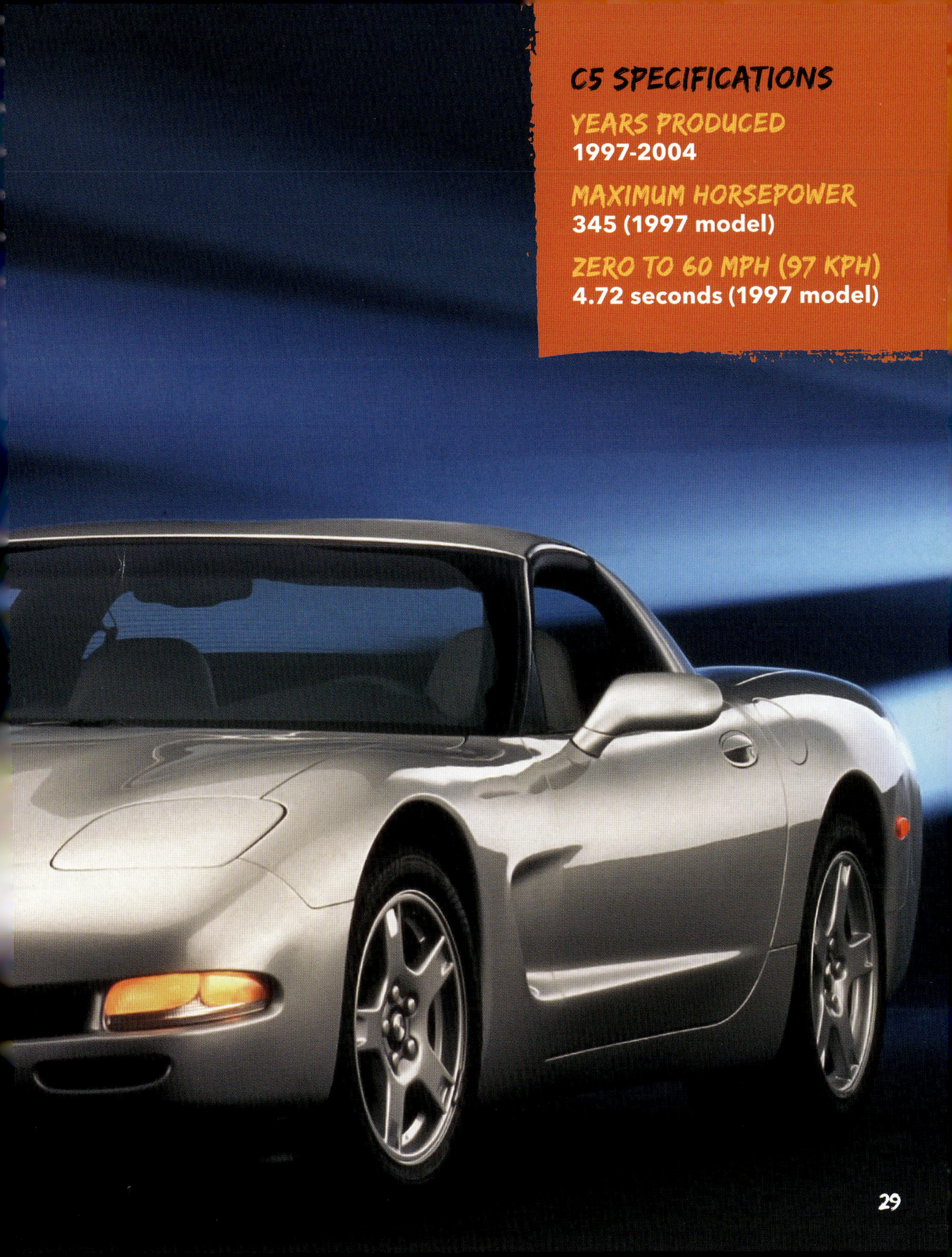

C5 SPECIFICATIONS

YEARS PRODUCED
1997-2004

MAXIMUM HORSEPOWER
345 (1997 model)

ZERO TO 60 MPH (97 KPH)
4.72 seconds (1997 model)

CHAPTER 9

SIXTH GENERATION

The C6 generation of Corvettes was Chevrolet's follow-up to the very successful C5 model. Minor flaws were fixed, and the ride improved. The body had a sharper, more chiseled appearance. Also, the C6 featured exposed headlights.

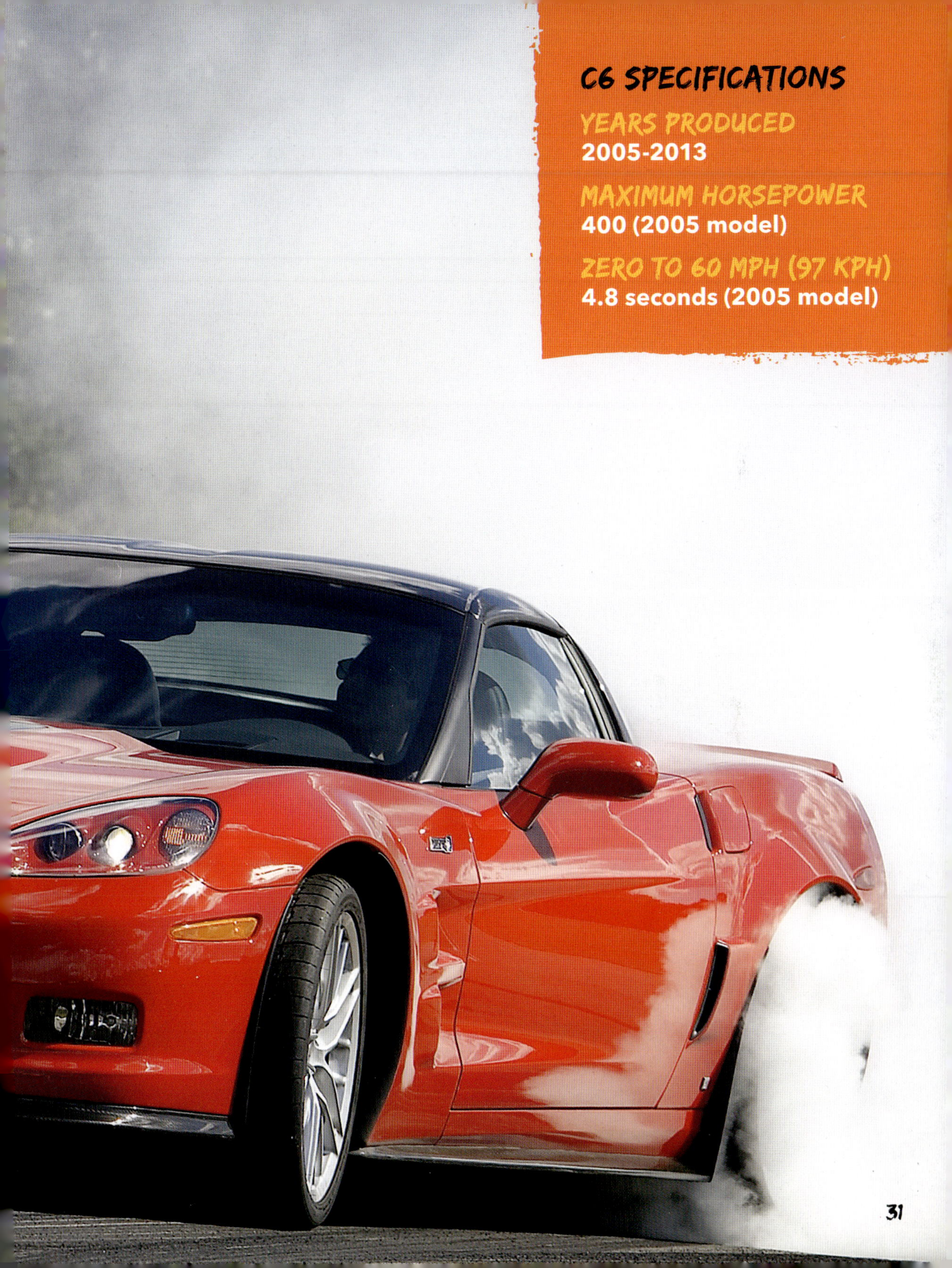

C6 SPECIFICATIONS

YEARS PRODUCED
2005-2013

MAXIMUM HORSEPOWER
400 (2005 model)

ZERO TO 60 MPH (97 KPH)
4.8 seconds (2005 model)

CHAPTER 10

SEVENTH GENERATION

The C7 Chevy Corvette Stingray was another step up in Corvette design. It featured a new LT1 V-8 engine. It produced more power while using less fuel. Computer-aided design resulted in an **aerodynamic** exterior that kept the Stingray stable at high speeds.

C7 SPECIFICATIONS

YEARS PRODUCED
2014-2019

MAXIMUM HORSEPOWER
450 (2014 model)

ZERO TO 60 MPH (97 KPH)
Under 4 seconds (2014 model, GM estimate)

CHAPTER 11

EIGHTH GENERATION

The introduction of the C8 Corvette Stingray in 2020 saw a rebirth of America's sport car. Redesigned from the ground up, the car has a chiseled, futuristic shape. It has a sense of power and speed, yet it unmistakably looks and feels like a Corvette.

C8 SPECIFICATIONS

YEARS PRODUCED
2020-present

MAXIMUM HORSEPOWER
495 (2020 model)

ZERO TO 60 MPH (97 KPH)
2.9 seconds (2020 model)

The C8 Corvettes feature a mid-engine design. The next-generation LT2 V-8 engine is placed just behind the cockpit. It produces an astonishing 495 **horsepower**, the most of any Corvette. A glass panel on the rear hatch shows off the new engine like a jewel in a showcase.

LT2 V-8 engine

XTREME FACT

Mid-engine cars have more weight in the back, which means more power is directed to the rear wheels. This results in more acceleration and better road-gripping traction.

The eighth-generation Corvette Stingray's engine is coupled to an eight-speed, dual-clutch automatic **transmission**. This combination gives the car sustained

road power. It also results in incredible acceleration. The C8 Corvette can go from 0 to 60 miles per hour (97 kph) in 2.9 seconds!

XTREME FACT

On a race track, the C8 Corvette Stingray's top speed was clocked at 194 miles per hour (312 km/hr).

The cockpit inside the C8 Corvette Stingray has been redesigned for better visibility. Buttons and gauges are easy to use. The squared-off steering wheel gives a good view of the digital dashboard display. Sporty seats hug the driver and passenger.

Audio
Phone
Nav
Wi-Fi Hotspot
Users
Settings
Apple CarPlay
Android Auto
70°/1:11
SYNC
AUTO
A/C
MAX
REAR

CHAPTER 12

CORVETTE UPGRADES

A 2015 Corvette Z06

The Corvette usually has three main upgrades available. They include the Z51, Z06, and ZR1 packages. Z06 and ZR1 Corvettes have more powerful engines, grippier tires, robust braking, and better suspensions. These upgrades make them ready for track racing.

CHAPTER 13

THE FUTURE

The 2022 C8 Corvette will likely have a Z06 upgrade. It may include a **turbocharged** V-8 engine with more **horsepower**, wider tires, a stiffer suspension, and powerful brakes. The Corvette is a road beast that has earned the right to be named "America's sports car."

XTREME CHALLENGE

TAKE THE QUIZ BELOW AND PUT WHAT YOU'VE LEARNED TO THE TEST!

1) What is a nickname for a Corvette?

2) What was the code name for General Motors' secret effort to build the first Corvette?

3) What is the Corvette automobile named after?

4) The first-generation Corvette began production in 1953. How many were sold that first year?

5) The body panels of Corvettes are made of which strong, lightweight material?

6) Where is the engine placed inside the C8 Corvette, and what is this arrangement called?

7) What is the main advantage for purchasing a Corvette Z06 or ZR1 upgrade package?

GLOSSARY

aerodynamic – Something that has a shape that reduces the drag, or resistance, of air moving across its surface. Sports cars with aerodynamic shapes can go faster because they don't have to push as hard to get through the air.

concept car – A car made to show off new designs or technology. Often exhibited at car shows to measure customer reaction before a decision is made to mass produce the vehicle.

coupe – A passenger car with a fixed roof that cannot be removed, usually with two or three doors. Coupes usually have a sportier look than four-door sedans, with a sloping rear roofline.

cylinder – A hollow chamber inside an engine where air and gasoline vapor mix. When ignited by a spark plug, the air/gas mixture explodes, forcing a metal piston inside the cylinder downward. The motion of the piston turns the gears that make the car move.

horsepower – A unit of measure of power. The term was originally invented to compare the power output by a steam engine with that of an average draft horse.

independent suspension – A system of springs and other devices that lessens the impact when a wheel hits a bump. In independent suspension systems, one wheel on an axle is not affected by the other wheel. This results in a smoother ride and better road handling.

transmission – A set of gears and shafts that transmits power from the engine to the axles, where the wheels are located.

turbocharger – A device that uses exhaust gases to power a compressor that injects additional air into the engine cylinders. With this added oxygen, more fuel can be added, resulting in more power.

ONLINE RESOURCES

Booklinks
NONFICTION NETWORK
FREE! ONLINE NONFICTION RESOURCES

To learn more about Chevrolet Corvettes, please visit abdobooklinks.com or scan this QR code. These links are routinely monitored and updated to provide the most current information available.

INDEX